Reflections of the Brazos Valley

Butterfly on lantana
Brazos County

Falls on the Brazos
Falls County

Reflections of the Brazos Valley

D. Gentry Steele & M. Jimmie Killingsworth

Texas A&M University Press *College Station*

Manufactured in China by Everbest Printing Co.
through Four Colour Imports

First edition

The paper used in this book meets
the minimum requirements
of the American National Standard
for Permanence of Paper
for Printed Library Materials, Z39.48-1984.
Binding materials have been
chosen for durability.
∞

LIBRARY OF CONGRESS CATALOGING-IN-PUBLICATION DATA

Steele, D. Gentry.
Reflections of the Brazos Valley / D. Gentry Steele and M. Jimmie Killingsworth.—1st ed.
p. cm.
ISBN-13: 978-1-58544-615-5 (cloth : alk. paper)
ISBN-10: 1-58544-615-7 (cloth : alk. paper)
1. Brazos River Valley (Tex.)—Pictorial works. 2. Landscape—Texas—Brazos River Valley—Pictorial works. 3. Natural history—Texas—Brazos River Valley—Pictorial works. 4. Brazos River Valley (Tex.)—Description and travel. I. Killingsworth, M. Jimmie. II. Title.
F392.B842S74 2007
976.4—dc22 2007003203

Bluebonnets, paintbrushes, and oaks
Washington County

Carolina wren at yard birdbath
Brazos County

Contents

Reflections of the Brazos Valley

Urban Park
Brazos County

Rivulets carved in sand after a rainstorm
Brazos County

Reflections from the Heart of Old Texas

BY M. JIMMIE KILLINGSWORTH

I live in College Station, Texas, making my home in an urbanless suburb. *Suburb* means to surround a city, so an urbanless suburb is something like a motherless child. Only here there was never any mother, never a city, only the gigantic university where I teach, Texas A&M, and these orphaned suburbs that spread out on every side like a Texas river at flood stage. Our skyline is the football stadium and the meteorology building. On the north side of campus, the strip shopping centers, apartment complexes, and housing developments run seamlessly into the town of Bryan, the seat of Brazos County, a once-prosperous farming and banking center that oil and cotton threaten

Kyle Field
Brazos County

to abandon altogether, leaving it to share what is now the main economy of the county, the export of higher education.

Texas A&M must be the largest university ever built in a cow pasture. It was built here for a reason. When the federal government handed out the money for the land-grant universities beginning with the Morrill Act in 1862, it required that schools supported by the funds address the practical problems of the day by channeling expert energy into the agricultural and mechanical disciplines—hence the A&M. Since then, the university has spread beyond those original streams of specialization, and that's one of the reasons I'm here, professing the more esoteric topics of rhetoric and literature.

The place where the university resides reflects its original purpose. The middle valley of the Brazos River was the first agricultural heart of Texas, the center of the land that Stephen F. Austin chose to start his famous colony. Austin called the Brazos Valley "as good in every respect as man could wish for, land first rate, plenty of timber, fine water—beautifully rolling."

Most travelers to the region and even many long-time residents might scratch their heads over Austin's claims for its beauty. Was the great Empresario's comment a ploy to draw respectable planters to his colony, something less than truth in advertising? Or has once-impressive land suffered from decades of overplanting and drilling and human development?

Maybe a little of both, I'll concede. But I also think we must learn to look with different eyes to see what Austin saw, or discover our own appreciation of this land. We might have to get off the highway—and sometimes abandon even the chuck-holed backroads, leaving the beaten path with its edges uprooted by feral hogs and armadillos and its middle dotted with the contemptuous scat of the raccoon and coyote. Follow faint trails made by the soft steps of deer and possum and get down to the muddy riverside to find the characteristic beauty of the place.

I started my life in a South Carolina mill village named for a river feature. Old Mr. Ware built his mill on the fast water of the big Saluda, harnessed the power, and called the place Ware Shoals. It's almost a ghost town now that the textile industry has moved to the Far East and the mill has burned down. Long before the town died and before memory set in for me, however, my parents had moved to the larger city of Greenville on the smaller Reedy River, looking for opportunity and a better place to raise the kids. What I remember from my boyhood is that, when we made visits back to the kin who stuck close to the dying town, crossing the Saluda River bridge meant that the drive to Ware Shoals—forty miles that seemed interminable to a restless child—was almost over. By the time I was grown, the old people in my family had all died or moved away, like most everybody else there. But the last time I checked, the river was still foaming over the gray rocks.

I went to college in Knoxville, Tennessee, on the banks of another big river that lent not only character but power and light to the whole region, thanks to the hydroelectric dams that the Tennessee Valley Authority built up and down the river's great length.

I took my first job as an English professor in Socorro, New Mexico, where the Rio Grande leaves a strip of green earth in a rifted valley with high red desert on both sides.

I taught two years in Memphis, where the Father of Waters divides the continent.

Finally in 1990, the restless mobility of the American economy deposited me in the valley of the Brazos River, and here I've settled.

Fifteen years doesn't sound like a long-term residency to heart-of-Texas natives, or to the serious natives of most any place. But after moving from school to school in the academic imitation of corporate life—moving on to move up—my decade and a half in the Brazos Valley turns out to be the longest time I've ever spent in one place in my fifty-plus years of life. No wonder the place starts to feel like home.

It didn't feel that way at first. After the Saluda, the Tennessee, the Rio Grande, and the Mississippi, I found the Brazos and its humid valley relatively unimpressive. I made a point of leaving often, seeking a more dramatic version of natural beauty. I returned to the bright color and edgy starkness of New Mexico whenever I could, or visited my wife's family near the Golden Gate and the redwood forests. I spent a week every summer with my own family on the beaches of the Carolina Grand Strand.

But as I settled, uprootedness gave way to reluctant tendrils of attachment. My daughter, Myrth, grew up here. My wife, Jackie, and I put in a garden, then another, and planted trees and bulbs and sprigs of vine until real roots formed.

The subtlety of the place appeals to me more and more. Nature doesn't always explode onto the scene or crawl up to your yard in the Brazos Valley. It can be subtle to the point of near invisibility. The Great Plains to the north shrink to prairies down here, and though the islands of post-oak woods expand with the swell of the rivers, the trees never attain the stature of their cousins to the east. We have some gentle uplifts in the hills and ridges around Brenham and Round Top, but they lack the obvious drama of cliffs and gorges. The swampiness of bottomland hints at the expanse of marshland farther south toward the Gulf, where the waterfowl and migratory birds gather in force, attracting bird watchers from all over the world. Our little wetlands never venture far from the rivers. They hold a limited attraction even for water birds.

Sometimes you have to look a little harder to find what you need when the heart cries out for relief from work, television news, and the predictability of air-conditioned life.

The subtlety of Brazos Valley scenery is a favorite topic of the photographer Gentry Steele, whose work has inspired me to adjust my eyes to the pleasures of the place and find words for my favorite images. The land here is not like the power places, as Gentry calls them—Niagara Falls, the Grand Canyon, the Yosemite Valley, the Big Bend, even Enchanted Rock. Those places provide everything the eye can handle; they fill up any frame you can imagine; they sate the mind. They have satisfied what can only be called a spiritual need for generations of human beings stretching back before recorded history. The ancient peoples left signs to show their appreciation—rock drawings, carved stones, the leavings of common campsites. In recent history, we've made parks, given tours, printed brochures and travel guides, written poems and taken photos for postcards and scrapbooks. The people keep coming, recharging their spiritual batteries.

Cutbank of stream
Brazos County

But I often wonder, what happens when we go home? What gets lost between nature in the grandest sense and the neighborhoods where we live our daily lives?

Gentry says that in places like the Brazos Valley, you sometimes have to bring something with you to the landscape—a desire, a memory, a different set of eyes. You can't come with an empty soul and expect to be filled up the way you can at the power places. The scenery here is subtle, the edges indefinite, requiring the right season or some special light on just the right day. You have to focus and refocus. His photographs are exercises in this way of looking, finding, framing, recording, remembering.

What he says reminds me of the time I went to summer camp when I was eleven years old. The South Carolina Education Association ran a science camp in the far northwestern corner of the state, where the streams that turned the textile mills flow out of the rich wet foothills of the Appalachians. My week there was like a dream—swimming in the cold mountain lake and canoeing in the creeks that fed it, learning how to turn over rocks and look carefully in just the right places to find snakes and salamanders, writing in a little notebook everything I could find in the modest library and everything I could observe about dragonflies, my assigned project that week. When my parents came to pick me up, I surprised them and the camp officials by begging to stay for another week. I recall hollering with delight when they all said yes. The counselors made me a pet and bragged to everyone about my notebook, which kept getting thicker with the details of dragonfly life.

After two weeks at science camp, I spent a week with my grandparents in Ware Shoals. I looked upon the old familiar yard full of Granny's overflowing flowerbeds and fragrant shrubs with new eyes. One thing I noticed like never before was the abundance of insect life. My grandfather helped me rig up a net and brought home some carbon tetrachloride from his drugstore to make a killing jar. I pinned my specimens—including a huge tiger swallowtail butterfly—in old cigar boxes. I spent all my days under the sunshine in the yard or walking in the nearby woods of pines and oaks and gums along the ridges and creeks leading down to the big river.

I loved nothing more than a creek in those days, looking for unusual rocks and animals along the edges, exploring flotsam and jetsam for lost treasures, and splashing right down the middle in dry shallow seasons, then leaving my canvas sneakers on a sunny bank to dry while I would sit with a friend and talk for hours about the secrets of the universe.

It all came back to me one sunny afternoon in the Brazos Valley, crashing with Gentry Steele through a dense understory of yaupon, cedar, and cat briar. We'd found an overview of an interesting gully west of College Station. A nice-sized creek had cut the beginnings of an oxbow in a thick patch of post-oak woods. He liked the light and wanted to get the camera down closer to the deep cut of the creek. We walked along the edge of the woods until we found a small opening, the path of hogs or deer, then put our heads down and broke on through. I don't remember wearing a hat when I was a kid, but I was glad to have one on this excursion. It worked like a helmet as we burrowed into the creekside woods.

Finally we made it down and got into position. Gentry was seated, bent into a yoga-like posture near the edge of the last embankment, his eye glued to the viewfinder. I squatted a little lower down the bank holding branches and brush out of the way of the camera's eye. The eye was focused on the place where the afternoon sun broke through the oaks, elms, and cedars to illuminate the subtle rust-and-cream colors of the creek bed and the exposed layers of clays on the opposite bank. The broken light played beautifully. The blue sky loomed above.

"I'm in heaven," Gentry said.

I've gradually learned that every time Gentry goes out, he brings more than the camera to the landscape—more than his long experience of making pictures and inquiry into the philosophy of photography, more than a lifetime of studying the land itself as an archaeologist, geologist, and biological scientist. He brings memories. When I mention my youthful love of creeks as we are driving away, he confesses to the same and tells me how he was lucky enough to make a livelihood from it, first as an amateur paleontologist—a fossil-hunting lad in south Texas who had his first acknowledgment in a scientific article at age fifteen—and then as a professional.

With his memories comes a love of the land—this land. "The Brazos Valley has been very good to me," he says. He made a successful career as a professor at Texas A&M, and he also made some of his greatest discoveries right here in the place we call home.

Following a hint he gave me, I made a trip a couple of days later to the Brazos Valley Museum of Natural History in Bryan. There I saw a photo spread from 1983. In one picture, a younger, bearded Gentry squats in an archaeological site next to a younger version of our A&M colleague David Carlson. Looking up at the camera, they're grinning—with good reason. Beside them lie the newly uncovered fossilized bones of a Late Pleistocene mammoth, the big ancestor of the elephant that once roamed the prairies of our valley. The bones had been exposed in a cutout of the Brazos, a gift from the river. Behind the two professors, the brown water laps, ready to reclaim the neatly flattened muddy ground of the site when the work is done.

In another shot, Gentry and Dave, joined by a couple of students, are hoisting the tusk of the mammoth up the steep bank of the river on what looks like an army medic's stretcher. Shirtless, his wiry muscles taut, Gentry with his corner of the load leads the way with a look back over his shoulder at the precious cargo. I've seen that look before on the faces of mothers in the driver's seats of big cars, checking on kids in car seats behind them. There's business in that look, but there's also love and a myriad of emotions known only to the looker.

Now, every time Gentry goes to the creek, he brings all of that with him, and when he looks through the camera's eyepiece into the dappled water of a creek in the late afternoon sun, he's not only in this little backwater of the Brazos Valley. He's in heaven.

Paintbrushes and bluebonnets in urban pasture

My brother from Atlanta came for a visit recently. He's used to having ten-lane interstate highways take him wherever he wants to go in a range of commercial development that sprawls almost unbroken from his Georgia home to Boston, Massachusetts. He flew into Houston's intercontinental airport, rented a car, and drove north on I-45. Still in his comfort zone.

But when he turned west on Texas 105, the highways narrowed and the pines thickened within a few miles. Before long, emerging into the alternating prairies and woodlands of river country, with nothing that he would call civilization in sight, he stopped to check his map. Locating himself at the right intersection—105 at Highway 6 near Navasota, in the heart of the Brazos Valley—he called me on his cell phone. "Man," he said, "you live in the boonies."

Later I told him that on my last trip to Houston, not far from the very spot he chose to make his call, I had to drive onto the shoulder to avoid a roadkilled feral hog so big it filled my entire half of the two-lane highway. It seemed a pretty fresh kill, but there was no sign of the vehicle that hit it. On my return trip, I noticed that somebody had dragged the dead monster off the road. Must have had a big truck to do that, one with a winch and tow chain. People love big trucks in the Brazos Valley—for a reason.

Brother felt more at home when he pulled into town and saw that we had a supply of city water, indoor plumbing, and plenty of franchise restaurants and discount stores. I warned him not to get too cozy. A few years ago, less than a half mile off the very road where he could see the bowling alley, the Post Oak Mall, and other signs of homogenized American culture, a friend of mine swerved to avoid another wild hog—a live one this time—and found himself upside down in his SUV. The car had rolled and hopped over a barbed-wire fence into a cow pasture. My friend escaped with his life and needed only a few stitches to mend his split scalp. As far as I know, that hog got away without a scratch.

The Brazos Valley begins a little south of Waco, near Marlin, Texas, in Falls County. There the big river that gives the region its name tumbles out of the north Texas limestone, thickens, and grows muddy in the deeper clays and soils of its middle range. There ends the part of the Brazos that John Graves immortalized in 1959 with his celebrated book *Goodbye to a River,* the wild part that "died" when the river was dammed north of Waco to make the big lakes for utility and recreation, boating and bass fishing.

The wedge of land below the falls of the Brazos at Marlin, through which the river flows in its southeastward trend toward the Gulf of Mexico, is a region of rich bottomland surrounded by bald prairies mixed with post-oak savanna and narrow streamside bands of taller trees and dense brush. A region small by Texas standards, crisscrossed by lesser streams and creeks, it remains mostly unknown to literary tourists and modern travelers. It has no interstate highways and no major cities.

Below the falls of the Brazos, the river has claimed a wide territory over the centuries, wandering and reshaping its softer, broader bed, curving smoothly and depositing fertile bottomlands sometimes ten miles wide up and down the region. This expansive valley continues south past Hempstead to San Felipe, where the even wider coastal plains spread out. It stops north of I-10, just shy of the big highway that carries a heavy human cargo from Houston to San Antonio and back again.

The eastern border lies somewhere just past the prairies rising from the floodplains of the Navasota River, a tributary of the Brazos, on the other side of which lie the Piney Woods of East Texas. The far western border might be the pine-fringed ridge that runs from Elgin to Bastrop. The rain that falls on the ridge drains westward into the Colorado River, eastward into the Brazos. On a clear day from the ridge at Elgin, you can see the Balcones Escarpment near Austin, where the famous Hill Country begins.

Between the falls and the coastal plains, north and south, and between the Piney Woods and the higher and drier Hill Country, east and west, the river defines the landscape. All the lesser waters seek it, raindrops and streams alike. It gathers them in its high, wide earthen banks and drives its muddy burden to the sea.

The river's full name is *Brazos de Dios,* Spanish for "arms of God." The origin of the name has been lost to history, but like everyone else who ponders the river with any interest, I have my theory of its original sense.

It goes like this: The early Spanish explorers and mapmakers followed the big rivers, the Brazos and the Colorado, from their outlet at the Gulf into the deepest core of the Texas country. They may have imagined the two big rivers as a powerful pair, the very arms of God embracing some of the finest farm land in all the new world. *Brazos* and *embrace* come from the same root word, and beyond a doubt the language fits the land. The hug of the great streams pulls all else toward them and gives the place its special character and local spirit.

The Spaniards discovered that the Brazos extends far up into the high country for its water, with fingers branching and reaching all the way to the plains west of the Palo Duro Canyon into what we now call New Mexico. But the heart of old Texas lies back nearer the place where the rivers find the sea, back in the broad breast of valleys between the arms of God, the land that Stephen Austin picked for his colony of planters and his dream of a civilized western country.

Austin got the land grant from the government of Mexico and founded the colony in 1822. He made his headquarters in the southern tip of the Brazos Valley at San Felipe, which was easily reached by boat. In fact, from Galveston, you could ride a steamboat all the way north to Washington-on-the-Brazos. It was there that the colonists eventually signed their declaration of independence from Mexico and took up arms against Santa Ana.

Washington lies at the confluence of the Brazos and Navasota rivers, the two streams that define the valley as we know it today. The rich land between the rivers attracted the Anglo American farmers who came to Texas in waves, the first arriving to make the Austin Colony a faster success than the Father of Texas had imagined, a second arriving after the United States annexed Texas in 1846. The often-troubled history of these people adds another kind of memory to give the Brazos bottomland the feeling of sacred ground.

If you travel east to west across the Brazos Valley, you leave a southern-gothic shadowland of pine and magnolia and head toward the drier open sky where Texas starts to feel like the American West of movie and legend. What lies between the Piney Woods and the Hill Country is a land that mingles south and west, in nature and in culture.

In the morning, you can hear the distinctive triplets of the Carolina wren on your backyard fence or the strangely descending *kuk-kuk-kuk* of another southern bird, the yellow-billed cuckoo in a pecan tree full of tent caterpillars, the bird that the old people call the rain crow. At midday, you might catch sight of the cuckoo's western cousin, the roadrunner, skittering along a pasture margin on the edge of town.

You can eat barbeque for lunch, and if you've taken your cholesterol medicine or gone for a jog in the humid heat, fill up again on enchiladas for supper. Driving home from work, you might see an oil well in a cotton patch. On a summer Saturday, you can start your day at the Navasota Blues Festival near the home of the legendary songster Mance Lipscomb, drive twenty miles north and listen to the bluegrass banjo at the Wellborn Community Center, and then, with a short ride of five miles more, end your day scuffing your boots to western fiddling and steel guitar at the Texas Hall of Fame in Bryan.

But the Brazos Valley remains an in-between place, hard to categorize as an attraction in a travel book or tourist guide. Like the snow geese and sandhill cranes whose annual flights mark the turning of the seasons in November and March, most tourists who happen into the region are flying through on their way to someplace else. Even the political history of Texas—the Austin Colony and the independence movement—passed through the Brazos Valley and mostly kept going. The government moved west to Austin. The flashy history of the Mexican War, the Indians' skirmishes with the Texas Rangers, and the great cattle drives claimed the attention of most historians and western literati. For the most part, you read the history of the Brazos Valley on roadside markers and in the names of the not-quite-town-sized communities, places like Washington and Independence. You can see that agriculture and oil thrived here once, but today they hang on mainly in remnants, leaving a larger history written in worn-out cotton fields and rusty implements—and in the big university. Now at Texas A&M, the practices of farming and engineering get refined in theory and research while pastures and fields in the College Station area give way to housing for students and professors. One big field that used to grow cotton west of town is now devoted to producing grass sod for lawns in new housing developments.

Despite the changes, though, nature won't be denied in the Brazos Valley. Just when you think the world will always be plain winter brown, springtime erupts into all shades of purple and scarlet—bluebonnets, Indian paintbrush, wine cup, red clover, Texas evening primrose. When you think the summer heat will never break, a blue norther splits the sky and sends thunderheads full with river-raising sheets of cold rain and jagged stalks of lightning. You may come to think your neighborhood is tame by any standards, and then, like one Texas A&M professor I know, wake up from an afternoon nap on an air mattress in your swimming pool, and discover you're sharing the air mattress with a four-foot water snake.

Coming home from an afternoon jog in the neighborhood, my daughter encountered a thick snake coiled in a corner of the entranceway to our house. The weather had been unusually rainy for the summertime, and the animals were apparently confused about property lines. She slipped inside and told my wife, who cracked the door and looked out. "It was a cobra," she told me later. Its head bobbed threateningly above the thick coil of its dark gray body, its neck cowled out behind the perilous head, fangs showing in front of a milk-white mouth ready to deal death to my entire household.

I checked to make sure that no cobras had escaped from the traveling circus or the local snake charmers and consulted the wisdom of my fisherman friend. Cottonmouth moccasins will act that way, he told me, spreading their considerable bulk even wider to enhance their threat. My neighbor across the street, whose swimming pool backs up to a drainage creek, tells me he pulls at least one cottonmouth per year out of the pool. My wife couldn't make it to her camera in time to get a picture before the big snake escaped into our hawthorn hedge and then, I guess, back to the creek by night, so the identification remained unsure. At least she didn't get bitten.

That is more than we can say for another woman we know in town. Stepping out to get her newspaper early one morning, she put her bedroom slipper down on a big gray snake that turned and bit her on the calf. She took it pretty well and managed not to swoon or die of a heart attack. Nor did she scream loud enough to wake her husband, so the snake got away. The doctor kept her under surveillance all day, then decided the bite wasn't poisonous. It must have been a Texas rat snake, he told her, an aggressive but nonpoisonous breed that often grows to six feet long. It likes to imitate the cottonmouth.

Later, after a hint from Gentry Steele and with the help of our local herpetologist, Toby Hibbitts, we were able to determine that the animal coiled on our porch was probably an eastern hognose snake. We had seen hognoses hunting the plentiful Gulf Coast toads around our pond. I had seen one of them expand the hood behind its neck slightly when sidling away from me on the street near our house. But they always had brown and tan markings. Toby showed us pictures of a dark "melanistic" phase of the adult snake, the coloring almost identical to the midnight gray of a cottonmouth. The mouth of the bluffing snake was shown wide open and cottony white in its threatening posture. He told us that a hognose will strike at you from the coiled posture, but will never even open its mouth. If the cobra act and the cottonmouth mimicry doesn't scare you away, the hognose will play dead, roll over and stiffen its body and dangle its tongue from its mouth. It will vomit and defecate so that it smells dead too.

One day Jackie fished a little hognose out of the pool skimmer. It was stiff as a pine plank. She laid it out on a tree stump in the sun for the rest of us to pay our respects. We admired its distinctive turned-up nose and its brown and tan coloration, lovely as inlaid wood on a fine musical instrument. Later she went out to bury it before the stink set in, but it was gone. Maybe a bird got it, she thought. The next morning she opened the garage door, and there beside the house, partially hidden by a little haw thorn shrub, was a brown and tan hognose, about nine inches long, looking up at her—if not the same snake, then its perfect twin. They locked eyes for the briefest moment before it slinked back into the greenery.

No wonder our serpents have a reputation for wiliness.

When I was going to college, back in east Tennessee, a friend of mine made an extended visit to Austin. On his return, we asked about the Texas countryside. "Trees are too short," he reported.

True enough. Driving west from the deep south, as your car emerges from the tall pines you've seen on and off all the way from Georgia to east Texas (your front grill now plastered with love bugs or mosquito corpses unless a hard Louisiana rain has shown up to provide a natural car wash), you first encounter the characteristic stunted oaks of Texas in the Brazos Valley. Post oaks that might have filled up your granny's yard in Tennessee have to grow in clumps here to make a decent shade. They barely attain half the height of their southeastern kin.

My neighbor Dan Lineberger, a horticulturalist who grew up in the Carolinas like me, says that the Texas trees stay short mainly to withstand periods of little rain, though the nutrients in the soil also limit growth. It's not unusual to have fifty inches of rain a year in our river country, but you learn not to count on when it's coming. The summer is usually dry, the winter wet, but not always. Droughts and down pours can catch you off guard in any season. Except for the prodigal cottonwoods and willows growing closest to the river, the trees play it safe and avoid overextending.

In the woods the post oaks mix with a few scruffy cedars and usually a fairly dense understory of yaupon holly (pronounced "yo-pon"). These small but handsome trees with their variegated bark, white and confederate gray, grow in thin-trunked clumps and produce bright red berries in winter. Their unfortunate scientific moniker is *Ilex vomitoria,* so named because their leathery evergreen leaves were used by the Indians to make a mildly intoxicating tea that allegedly produced an emetic effect when taken in high doses. Like the stunted oaks, the yaupon can tolerate times of drought and highly alkaline soils.

I suspect the trees seemed short to the settlers in the Austin Colony, too, since they mostly came from the trans-Appalachian south like my friend from Tennessee or my brother from Georgia. But I doubt the old colonists complained about the comparative beauty of the trees. They didn't come for the scenery; they came for the soil. They were glad for the plentiful timber to cut for burning and building, and the good bottomland for planting. It's said that Stephen Austin heard music in the sound of trees falling under the ax in the valley.

The first year of the Austin Colony ended badly. The people got the fields cleared and planted, but they failed to read the meaning of the trees. The summer drought destroyed their crops and left them in ruin. They retreated to the coast, only to come back, chastened and more cautious in the years to come.

On that account, the trees seem wise to me, and I begin to see their particular grace and apt beauty. When I go squinty-eyed in the hallucinatory heat of a summer day and see the oaks squatting in clumps at the edge of a prairie or standing alone in an old cleared field, I see something like a bonzai garden. Mother Earth keeps them trimmed by giving only the most necessary nutrients, and Father Sky threatens to withhold his rain if they grow too bold and proud. So they stay short and hug the ground. And they survive.

One thing I love about folk music—whether it's ballads brought over from the old world, African American country blues, or bluegrass—is the way the songs stay grounded in the places of their origin. Countless mining songs mention Harlan or Hazard, Kentucky; the old minstrel tunes recall the "land of cotton"; the blues tell of the hard life from Houston and Texarkana to Slidell and New Orleans; and cowboy songs take you back to Texas with lyrics ranging from the Red River Valley to the streets of Laredo.

Driving through the Brazos Valley one day, I was listening to a disk of roots music by a young string band called the Old Crow Medicine Show. I associated the group mainly with the Appalachians and heard references in their songs to Raleigh, North Carolina, and Johnson City, Tennessee. But then my ear caught a geographical allusion that surprised me—a reference to the place where the Brazos meets the Navasota River. How did these boys from back east come by these lines? I wondered. Must be an old Mance Lipscomb song that I somehow never heard. When I stopped to look at the credits on the liner notes, I saw the name of *Fuqua* beside the song. Further reading gave the names of the band members, including one Critter Fuqua.

That night, I visited the Web site for Old Crow Medicine Show in search of Critter Fuqua. I sent an e-mail asking about the origin of the song, mentioning that I was a college professor from Texas writing an essay about the Brazos Valley. The Web master wrote back and promised to have Critter himself get in touch with me. "Critter is a literary dude, too," the message revealed, "and a Texan." To date, I haven't heard from the young songster who, as it turns out, was writing of his own homeland even as he channeled the spirit of old Mance. I also found out that the Fuqua family left its name on a street in Houston.

Critter's song brought home a realization: I had never seen the actual place where the Brazos and the Navasota rivers come together.

So one fine cool Saturday in December, a clear bright day, Jackie and I set out to find the place. We drove down Highway 6 and exited to the town of Navasota just after crossing the river running diagonally under the road in its southwestern passage. On our way toward town, the river kept its distance, roughly parallel, gradually cutting through fields just to the north as the road curved a little south. We could tell where it was by a tall stand of cane, strong green stalks topped by flags of flaxen silk. I mentioned something I had read: We have a snake that specializes in that kind of terrain—the canebrake rattler.

We lost sight of the canebrake as we passed the big houses built from cotton money on the outskirts of Navasota and then passed through town, going roughly west toward Washington-on-the-Brazos, where the river seemed to be heading. We worried that the confluence would happen on private land, and we'd never see it.

Just before Washington, we crossed the river, the bottomlands spreading out wider than before, and soon we saw why. The Brazos itself appeared in no time at all, less than a quarter mile away. We were close to where the rivers meet, and here we could see very well how, to a mind shaped by agriculture, this country could hardly be better—the wide floodplains of two good rivers joining to form a wedge of rich soil, plentiful water, stands of timber on all sides, a growing season that spans from February to November—impressive breadth in both space and time.

We came into the town of Washington, where all that's left is a few ruined buildings. When river traffic gave way to the railroad, the town was bypassed and never recovered except as a state historic park and popular site for viewing wildflowers in the spring. We stopped briefly by the old bridge, now closed and blocked by a big wooden barrier and a bramble thicket—humanity and nature saying no. We craned our necks but saw only the Brazos, the water running high and hard, muddy and reddish-brown in the bright sun.

We pushed on to the state park and asked the ranger there about the rivers' meeting place. No problem, she told us; you can see it from the river overlook on the park trail.

On foot, we made our way. Last spring, we had walked this very trail, but like most tourists, we more or less ignored the river and the sky because the bluebonnets had our attention. This is one of the favorite places in all of Texas for viewing the famous state flower. The showy dark blue blossoms, mixing with the orange of the Indian paintbrush and the delicate pink of the Texas evening primrose, turn the park meadows into a continuous show of bright color in April, filling the eye too completely to allow for other scenic opportunities. We often see our neighbors down here, but we've also met tourists from as far away as Japan and Australia.

Now it is winter, though, the bluebonnets gone. We cross an earthen dam that makes a small pond from one of the creeks running down to the Brazos. The ranger told us that the beavers had come back in recent years. We don't see them, but a low-flying V of snow geese reminds us of the season. Ducks rise in the distance, and a small group of cormorants streams by overhead, backed by the crystalline blue of the big sky.

We see some hog sign—the soil furrowed and rooted—along one of the trails. A ranger told us later that he's met the creatures themselves when he takes his every-morning walk on the trails. I didn't ask him if he felt the same as a fellow I met

once in Tennessee, who told me that he wasn't afraid of black bears at all, but if he met a wild boar in the trail, he would "climb a sapling and make it stand up."

We arrive at the river overlook, two benches arranged behind a light wooden barrier, the big riverside cottonwoods rising on both sides. And there it is. On the last point of land between the two rivers—the great mass of the Brazos with its high water overwhelming the narrower Navasota—stands a great blue heron. From its peninsular perch, it can select fish from either river.

The water from the Navasota is a different color, a rich forest green. Just below Lake Limestone, I have read, it ranks as one of the most polluted rivers in Texas. From there it passes through a natural filtration system of oak forests and grassy fields. With its low banks, it spills its water frequently along the way. By the time it reaches the Brazos, it is relatively clear despite having picked up some new silts and agricultural runoff. It may still be polluted for all I know, but you can't tell from looking. The color is beautiful—Robin Hood green.

We can see the darker water like a shadow where it enters the sunny northeast side of the Brazos, across the river from the overlook. It makes green paisleys and commas and dark cirrus drifts in the reddish chocolate of the Brazos. Within a couple of hundred yards, it is gone, fully incorporated into the wide current and shoreline swirls of the big river, whose power we find inspiring on this clear day at the end of a year of record rain.

We're drawn to the river, so we step around the barrier and climb down the high bank to the muddy flats. The soft mud slips beneath the dead cottonwood leaves that make a false floor. Looking down in the mud, we see the perfect tracks of a raccoon that had been here on its nightly rounds. A pileated woodpecker comes across the river screaming, his red crest high, black and white wings spread wide. It's as big as a crow, so we take its warning seriously. We head back up the bank and, as best we can, follow the calling bird in its erratic flight to a big dead tree near the visitors center.

A month later, I return to find the Brazos running a little lower. At the point of entry, the Navasota asserts itself more definitely in the combined stream, forming a forest-green lane down the far side, gradually narrowing but staying relatively intact for as far as I can see. I'm told that the smaller river can maintain its identity for a full mile in some seasons.

Besides the excitement of finding the place mentioned in Critter Fuqua's song, I cannot say why I am attracted to the confluence of the two rivers. It has something to do with bearing witness to one version of life's passage that the poet Walt Whitman called "the merge." The tributary merges with the river, the river with the sea, as our own lives merge with one another's and eventually, in death, with nature again.

If young Mr. Fuqua intended to invoke something of his homeland with what can only be a nickname, he chose well. Critters abound in these parts. But they have so many hiding places in the wetlands, brush clumps, prairie grasses, and oak woods that too often the only way an ordinary citizen encounters them is dead on the highway.

Roadkill is abundant. An A&M student told my colleague that on a single trip from College Station to Houston—a mere ninety miles—she and her friend counted more than 200 animals sacrificed to the convenience of modern travel. She may have been exaggerating—Texans are known for it—or she may have included mice, voles, small birds, and grasshoppers in her count. But if not in number, her observation was true enough in spirit. There's a lot of roadkill on Texas highways.

I know a place on Wellborn Road in College Station that, like certain intersections in human travel, tends to incur an especially large number of animal fatalities. Hardly a week passes without my seeing a fresh kill—mostly raccoons, but sometimes a possum, skunk, or snake, often lying right alongside an earlier fatality that has not yet decomposed or been cleaned up by the crows and vultures. The place is not far from my house. I go by every day on the way to work.

One late afternoon I walked down to the spot to take a closer look. Just before I arrived at the fatal intersection, I passed a clump of oak and yaupon, one of the last remaining lots of undeveloped land in the neighborhood. I remember that just a few years ago, before the town houses across the street were built on the old prairie and the clump of woods was a little larger, I met a white-tailed doe coming out of these oaks. I don't think she lived in there, but she was definitely feeding and may have been looking for water. It was summer, and there was a drought that made the animals stray from their usual ranges. The trail she used, a little too small for humans, is still there, not yet overtaken by the yaupon shrubs, but it won't be long. I wonder if the trail will close before the woods are removed in the inevitable development of this property.

On this day, I pause only briefly and move on to the road. There's quite a lot of traffic. It's about 5:30 P.M., and people are headed home from work. I get to the end of the neighborhood street and turn right onto the dirt shoulder of the road. It's a good two-lane road with a turn lane in the middle and emergency lanes on either side. The place I'm looking for is only about twenty yards away. I stroll down and find a week-old raccoon corpse. I remember when it was a fresh kill, but now it is flat and nearly totally desiccated, despite the recent heavy rain. The stink is gone.

Not ten yards beyond the first is another raccoon pelt, even older and more torn up. Bits of fur stick in the grass, along with bits of trash thrown from careless cars.

I focus myself on this place. I follow the faint trail of the animals over to a utility easement parallel to the road, partially screened from the passing cars by a hedge of brush.

I stop directly between the oak clump and the degraded raccoon pelt on the road. I can barely make out the network of animal pathways. The one I follow runs from the site of the coon's fatal crossing back to the clump of woods. I remember the line from Gary Snyder's remarkable poem, "The Dead by the Side of the Road": "Our ancient sisters' trails/the roads were laid across and kill them."

The easement is lined on either side with lightweight trash that has blown over from Wellborn

Road and caught in the knee-high brush—foam cups and fast-food containers, plastic grocery sacks, and paper rotted down to tissue thinness. These human traces are harder for the earth to reconcile than the subtle leavings of other animals, even their very skins.

The dusk is growing. I walk a little farther from the road into another grassy opening, the stunted oaks lifting their heads above yaupon thickets on either side. Ahead of me is the subdivision of ranch-style houses, my own neighborhood, which has flooded the whole prairie except for this tiny island of woods. A mourning dove bursts up from the soft purplish grass and careens off into the woods on my left, a sunset patch of pink showing under the wing.

I stand still. At first I don't notice the bright red berries on the yaupon. The color seems to emerge into clear view only when I stand still, focus, and breathe slowly. Then I wonder how I could have missed the berries; they're practically shining like bright beads in the failing light of day. I remember that Christmas is little more than a week away. The patch of woods is decked out in red and green. Now I hear the chirping of the sparrows in the grass, the chickadees up in the oaks. I nearly forget the roar of the cars and trucks on the road behind me, the people heading home from work. On the railroad tracks that run parallel to the road on the other side, a freight train is coming. I feel the vibrations through my boots on the ground, but fail to prepare for the blast of the whistle. My shoulders clinch and the hair stands up on the back of my neck.

I wonder if this is the way it was for the raccoon whose pelt is now rotting on the road. One night, when the traffic was much diminished if not gone, it left the bigger woods on the far side of the railway, crossed the shrinking pasture, then the train tracks and the road. Maybe it lost itself in the clump of yaupon and oak and, like me, forgot the noise of the cars, found something good to eat and made itself at home. At the first hint of dawn, it bestirred itself and walked unthinkingly along the faint animal trail and, suddenly feeling the hard asphalt under the pads of its feet, looked up too late to do anything more than freeze in the beam of predawn headlights bearing down, fur rising for the last time on the back of its neck.

I glance back one more time at the pelt by the road. I take one more look at the red berries on the yaupon, now barely discernable in the growing dark. As I walk home, the Christmas lights are coming on in the neighborhood. I remember the end of Snyder's poem: "night-shining eyes/The dead by the side of the road."

I take a little comfort in knowing that I'm not the only one interested in roadkill. Gentry Steele, my partner in this project, was once known among his students as the Roadkill King. His interest is somewhat more scientific than mine. Teaching courses that require a deep knowledge of animal anatomy and behavior can be hard when most of the animals in our region have learned to survive by leading a primarily nocturnal existence. People are most active during the day, leaving the nighttime safer for the prowling of raccoons, possums, rabbits, deer, hogs, mice, snakes, and toads. What we know of animal life from daytime observations is limited mainly to birdwatching. With the gift of flight, birds can stay clear of people, at least unarmed people, by flying out of reach. Even so, I do occasionally find some birds whose flight paths have intersected fatally with the grills of automobiles and the glass and steel of our university buildings. Migration is especially perilous. I have mourned a number of warblers in their new spring plumage dead on the ground outside my office building on campus, the windows having proved impenetrable.

Gentry has used roadkill as a window into the life of nocturnal animals. He has studied skeletons collected on the highway and taken the census of competing animals, such as coons and possums, by collecting and counting dead things on the road. He also schedules fieldwork for the early morning and late afternoon, when the live animals are sometimes observable. Relatively dark days can also be revealing. One rainy morning in winter, I met a raccoon trying to stay dry by taking a short cut through a dimly lit parking building. Gentry made a nice series of photographs of a toad sampling the light from the shadowy safety of a rocky hole.

I have a friend who's an accomplished bicyclist. Once he rode all the way from Austin to New York City. He lived for a while in College Station and took the four-lane bypass to work at the university every day, using the wide emergency lane to stay clear of the car and truck traffic.

One day he was riding home in the early evening, about twilight time, and saw what appeared to be a large black dog ahead of him, running alongside the emergency lane on the flat, unpaved ground of the raised roadbed. As he overtook the animal, he was surprised to see that it was a fair-sized pig, maybe a hundred pounds or a little more. The thing never broke stride but turned a wary eye up at the cyclist briefly before redoubling its speed. If either one of them had swerved left into the traffic, somebody would have ended up as roadkill.

But my friend made the pass successfully and lived to tell it. He said he had to pedal hard to pull away.

"What were you thinking when you were side by side with the pig?" I asked him.

He said, "I was wishing I could run that fast."

Driving north out of Bryan, we head to the falls of the Brazos, the northern opening of the valley. We follow Highway 6, which carries the main north–south traffic through the region, running all the way from Waco to Hempstead, a stream of humanity, steel, and horsepower that stays parallel to the big river but never gets close enough for travelers like us to see, that space reserved to this day for grazing and planting. We take the Marlin exit, and after a few miles through old cotton country, including a wet field with a wintering flock of sandhill cranes and a prison farm named for a former governor, we find the modest county park at the site of the falls.

At the end of the short road through the picnic ground and campsites, the falls come into view. It's

high water when we arrive, a strong current. The concrete crossing built over the falls is completely covered by the abruptly falling river that drops a few feet, then swirls and foams onto a ledge of limestone, creating a brisk run of white water. The turbulence fairly quickly subsides as the river digs into the muddy soils that form its bed all the way to the sandier land of the coastal plains. After no more than a hundred yards, the water recovers its stately flow.

It's not Niagara, but its width and power still manage to impress. We know the river's determination, how it maintains a more or less constant breadth and volume all the way down the valley. We know that the relatively clear green color it displays up here—more like the Navasota down below—will yield to the muddy chocolate we've seen in places like Washington-on-the-Brazos as it scoops up soil and patiently molds the land.

On a short walk, we soon exhaust the limits of the park. The wind whips as we cross the bridge over the river just north of the falls. The strong current has left a huge pile of jetsam against each of the concrete abutments. Uprooted trees, logs, even an entire johnboat are in various stages of being dismantled by the rush of the water. We pitch sticks into the river to watch them run.

The water and the wind seem to be the main animating forces on this winter day. I see wisps of dirty gray fiber fluttering in the breeze around the desiccated corpse of a skunk stuck in stiff blades of winter grass—signs of the lingering cotton trade in these parts left by trucks carrying product to market. On the little road down to the river, we find the almost perfectly preserved skeleton of a small dog, dumped here dead no doubt, but flattened by subsequent traffic and picked clean by crows and other carrion eaters. In an earlier stage of decay is a goat beneath the bridge. I've found animal remains on river access roads all over Texas. I guess the idea is to dump the dead things and hope the river will carry them someplace else—the afterlife maybe.

There's mistletoe all over the trees, and since it's close to Christmas, we decide to gather a little. I find an old board and, by throwing it javelin-like into the overhead branches, try to knock loose a good-sized bunch. I'm able to get a nice sample with the translucent berries. I start to call out to Jackie in victory but notice that she's collecting good samples at shoulder level.

We walk back and eat our lunch at the picnic ground overlooking the falls, admiring the big black willows bending out over the river. In one, a pair of gray and tan squirrels chase each other round and round the partially submerged trunk. Three anglers are working a small pool by the bank just below the falls, their genders indeterminate, they're so bundled up against the early December wind. They have at least six lines out in the water but catch nothing while we're watching. A man and a little boy carry their tackle down to the boat launch above the falls and sit in the sun with their backs against a low concrete wall. The boy in his car coat and red stocking cap cannot be more than five years old. Recalling the times I've carried unruly kids on fishing expeditions, I marvel at the patience of this child.

Except for the bright red of the cardinal flashing across our line of sight and an occasional quick view of the woodpecker's red nape, the birds here maintain a winter decorum in gray and blue. Even the warblers and goldfinches keep only a hint of yellow in the trim of their gray-flannel suits, as if to politely allow the bluebirds a chance to provide the main show of color.

An older fellow comes out of a camper and walks over to us. From the small talk, we gather that he's retired and has some time on his hands. Noticing the binoculars, he asks if we're birdwatchers and tells us that he's just learning. He points out the eastern bluebird. We tell him about a belted kingfisher whose bright blue feathers Jackie had sighted near a backwater pond of the creek that runs into the Brazos just below the falls. I had verified its laughing call coming across the water.

As we drive away after lunch, we see the man heading for the creek, shiny new binoculars in hand.

About 15 miles south of College Station, where the heart of the valley expands between the Brazos and Navasota rivers, lies the community of Millican. In our part of Texas, many of the places we euphemistically call *communities* were once thriving towns. By the time of the Confederacy, Millican reached a population of 3,000 residents, reputedly the largest town north of Houston. Rebel troops trained here, in numbers as large as 5,000. In those days, the town was the northernmost point for the railroad—which still runs parallel to the road I've followed to get here—and a focal point for the local cotton culture.

Today there are few signs that a town ever prospered here, but there's little doubt that King Cotton shaped the land. It reminds me of the Mississippi Delta, the wide flat fields spreading out on all sides, little cookie-cutter houses along the road set up on blocks over the marshy ground of the broad flood plain, trees left around the biggest houses for shade—post oaks, water oaks, live oaks, pecan, and elm. Farm workers still live in these wood-frame dwellings, their children and grandmas waving to me from the narrow porches. Their predecessors saw the plantation days give way to tenant farms and sharecropping. Then corporate agriculture took a turn, leaving its mark on road signs and even one community name: Allenfarms.

Agriculture now appears to hang on by a slender thread of economic opportunity. The old cotton gin stands at the center of the greatest concentration of buildings, still in operation, though trending toward rust and dust. Not more than half the land formerly plowed and tractored around here remains under cultivation. Some fields are used for pasture; others have lain fallow for years. Some show signs of more recent cultivation, old stalks of corn or sorghum bending in rough rows among the wild insurgency of weeds. The rodent population has steadily increased, if the birds of prey are any indication. The red-tailed hawks and other large raptors claim segments of land no more than a quarter mile wide. I see them posted on the fences or coasting over the weeded land at regular intervals. One of the hawks I see sports the dark phase of its coloring. It looks like a smallish golden eagle, feathers almost completely a rich burnished brown with bright highlights in the late afternoon sun.

The southward growth of College Station may eventually engulf the community of Millican, but not yet. For now, it bears the fading marks of the old plantation culture and the fickle history of transportation. Millican prospered as Washington-on-the-Brazos waned to the south, the railroad superseding the river traffic. After the Civil War, when the railroad extended to the north, Millican became one stop among many. Nature played a role in the town's demise, too, when yellow fever passed through in 1867. One year later, a nasty confrontation between post-Confederate vigilantes and newly freed African Americans brought the bloody history of Reconstruction to the Brazos Valley. Citizens died again, most of them black. Federal troops were needed to restore order, but brutal lynchings recurred from time to time until around 1930. Ironically, the black leaders who braved incidents like those in Millican, along with their Republican colleagues who were contemptuously labeled as scalawags and carpetbaggers in the post–Civil War South, voted to bring the land-grant college to our district under the Morrill Act. Without that modest beginning, we would never have had our big university.

Today the railroad that spurred the growth of Millican begins to look like an artifact. Passenger lines have been overtaken by air travel, freight trains compete only weakly, and often collaborate, with overland trucking via the highway system. Brazos Valley communities stay small mainly because they lie off the trail of the interstate highways, which all but define the outward boundaries of the region—I-45 to the east, I-35 to the west, I-10 to the south. With only one small airport connecting to Dallas and Houston and without an interstate highway cutting through, our valley remains an in-between place, a wedge of river-enriched land that history keeps forgetting and nature keeps reclaiming.

Nature tried to reclaim the water feature in my family's backyard. The previous owners of our College Station house had built a fish pond, but by the time we moved in, the exotic koi or goldfish popularly stocked in such water gardens had departed, leaving the pond to host a healthy spawn of native sunfish and a nice stand of umbrella grass. Jackie trimmed the tall grass, installed a new filtration system, and introduced some brightly colored koi. She made the feeding of the fish into a daily ritual for communing with the outdoors, morning and night every day of the year.

One night that first summer, a strange sound drew us into the yard. In the moonlight we could make out a whole community of toads. They grew quiet and sat still as we approached. But before we even reached the door on the way back in, their courtship had commenced again. Wild singing filled the air. Within a week, the sunfish were feasting on tadpoles, and Jackie found the discarded skin of a big brown water snake on the rocks beside the pond.

After a few months, though, she got frustrated with the superiority of the sunfishes' aggressive feeding skills and blamed them for the various diseases that kept killing the koi and, somewhat more disturbingly, for the mysterious disappearance of the smaller ornamental stock.

She calculated how much money she was losing on providing food for the sunfish and replacing the koi. Too much. She did not so much as sniff at my idea to forget the koi and let the sunfish stay and live by their own devices. She drained the pond, scooped up the offending perches in a bucket, put the bucket in the car, and dumped the contents in the pond by the police station, where the indigenous fish would have to compete with their own kind and stay clear of the ducks and local family fishing expeditions as well.

Then she refilled the pond and restocked it with koi of various sizes and colors. Disease and disappearance continued to plague the little fish, but the big ones got a foothold (or whatever you would call the same for a fish). For a while she was satisfied to let the big ones grow. One died from disease, but the other two thrived, and after a couple of years they have become an established element of our backyard ecology.

Last summer, she got the urge to raise little fish again, so she put three new ones in the pond. The next morning, I came home from an early coffee session to find the little dog barking her head off and my wife and daughter in their pajamas in the back yard. Myrth was pointing her camera at a round-bellied, brown-striped bird with a long, straight beak, perched on the power wire behind the house.

From the photo she took, we determined it was an American bittern, not big enough to make a meal of the large koi but well suited to feed on the small fry. The case of the disappearing fish was finally solved—the sunfish, now long gone, exonerated.

A few weeks later, I saw a young yellow-crowned night heron shopping the pond, no doubt wondering what happened to the breakfast buffet.

When the rains come fast and hard in the Brazos Valley, the waterways can threaten life and livelihood. A cultivated field will become a shallow lake in a matter of hours; roads will run like streams without regard to city limits and property lines.

In the summer of 2004, we had record rains at a time when we'd learned to expect dry weather. In fact, it was the third year in a row that June was particularly wet.

That year the Navasota and all the tributaries in the valley redefined their banks, and the Brazos threatened to overflow even its own high earthen vessel. North of Bryan, the town of Hearne suffered a great deal. The newspaper had an aerial photograph of cows practically swimming in their pastures. As their hooves sought their usual trails under several feet of water, they left wakes behind them. Some creatures had to resort to swimming, no doubt, and often it proved too much for them. I saw a pair of drowned pigs in the ditch by the road near Plantersville. Jackie and I saw another pair over in East Texas near Jasper. Why they died in pairs like that remains a mystery to us, although the Jasper couple appeared to be kin, a sow and her half-grown offspring.

One day after the rain had fallen for a straight week, Myrth walked out in the back yard and saw our neighbors, whom we never see because of the privacy fence that separates our properties, waving from their back patio. The low drainage between the yards was full and flowing—we call it "the river" at times like this. It had washed out the foundation of several fence posts and caused the community barrier to tumble.

"Something there is that doesn't love a wall," begins the Robert Frost poem "Mending Wall." In Frost country, up in New England, it's the winter ice that plays havoc with the stone fences between farms. Down here it's the river that at flood time wants to command the entire landscape.

Two days of early morning fog in late winter. On such days, it seems that the river is not satisfied to dissolve the boundaries we make in the land. It wants the very air itself.

The fog appears to confuse the animals in their crossings. I go out jogging through the dense air, unable to see the end of the lane, and on my return trip I find a raccoon, its head bloodied and eyes glazed over dead in the middle of the main north–south street of my neighborhood. Next day, the air equally thick, I jog close past a cottontail, freshly dead on Rock Prairie Road, its legs extended in final stride, no marks at all on its body, eyes still open and clear in the last stages of animation.

Humidity is the main reason I prefer winter excursions in the Brazos Valley. As early as March, you can feel the summer heat creeping in, the atmosphere beginning to boil. You go out to look at the bluebonnets and even a short nature walk can leave you sweaty. The mean annual humidity is over 80 percent—that's mean in both senses of the word.

History says that Houston, the largest city in our vicinity, was built on oil, but I doubt I'm the only person who's noticed that you can plot its growth alongside the development of air-conditioning technology. Without air conditioning, Houston would never have become the sprawling metroplex it is today.

Like most suburbanites in the region, my family depends on mechanical cooling for a season that might run from April to November. When the temperature rises and the world goes green, the air refuses to dry out. The "double nineties" is not uncommon: temperature pushing toward 100, humidity over 90 percent. Even when the temperature crosses the century mark, the humidity strives impossibly to catch up. And it holds the heat. Nights rarely cool down more than ten degrees.

In summer, you break a sweat going from air-conditioned office to air-conditioned car. A four-cylinder car won't work in this climate, according to an Englishman I know in town, because the engine won't drive the air conditioner fast enough. The smaller motor works well enough for me, and I do what I can to acclimate and enjoy the outdoors in every season, but I spend most of the summer damp—even when I'm not swimming.

Driving east out of College Station on Highway 30 toward Huntsville, you come to the Navasota River at a swampy point where the water seems never to remember where its banks ought to be. No human can count on this land staying dry enough to plant, so the swamp-resistant trees and the animals move in.

Here I've seen deer and hogs feeding at the damp edge of the water-oak and cypress woods. I've seen roadkilled coons, possums, skunks, and armadillos.

Less commonly I see a cottontail and, very rarely, a jackrabbit. My uncle back in South Carolina, who loved nothing better than running rabbits with his beagles, told me some years ago that the deer had overpopulated and driven out the rabbits. He told me of the decline sadly, shortly before his own death. I hope I do him justice when I say that a life without rabbits in the woods may not have been worth living for him. His house was the only place I was ever served meals of rabbit and squirrel on a regular basis. Now I couldn't name a single person who still hunts and eats the wild members of the rodent family once considered delectable, though my niece and her husband, who live in Bremond, right here in the Brazos Valley, raise domestic rabbits for meat.

Driving over the bridge on the Navasota today, I catch sight of something darting across the road. I slow down and see that it's a coyote out on this cool and cloudy midmorning. I pull over to watch it zigzag across the upward slope of the wet field on the east side of the river. Looking back over a shoulder, it catches sight of the car and stops to watch me. After a brief standoff, we move on, keeping an eye on each other as we go.

Coming to Panther Creek, I see no sign of cats but two caracaras come winging in. The distinctive black-and-white patterns on their wings and bodies attract my attention. Then I see their red faces and flat-crested heads that always remind me somehow of parrots. Their parallel flight divides, and I seem to catch the eye of one watching me through the windshield of my car.

The predators and the name of Panther Creek remind me of the tracks I saw a few weeks ago from the high embankment of a creek whose name I don't know. The prints were big and nearly round in the soft sand on the far edge of the water. I couldn't find a way down the bank to get a better look and had to settle for a view through the field glasses. Later at the natural history museum, I looked at the feet of a stuffed cougar for a long time. I wanted to be convinced.

Just past the community of Carlos on the east side of the Navasota, the evergreens make a play for dominance. Driving out Highway 30 from College Station, you first see an increase in the size and number of the cedars, then the occasional loblolly pine, and finally a serious stand of the tall trees, enough to make you think you've left the post-oak savanna for good.

But then it comes back. At Roan's Prairie, the land opens again into what seems to my untrained eye to be some good pastureland. Cattle roam across the winter-yellow grasses. In other fields, the plentiful hay is rolled and piled. Red-tailed hawks coast across from the black willows and hackberry trees by the creeks and lodge on the fence posts, the power lines, or the big trees standing alone in the fields. On ridges, wind-swept oaks point away from the direction of the prevailing southwest breezes. The country rolls and sweeps.

Finally, as you cross the San Jacinto River, east Texas begins in earnest. From the river bottom, you can see the next ridge covered with the tall, dark pines that mark the western edge of the Sam Houston National Forest. In five minutes' drive, you've left the land of the Brazos Valley.

After spending a few years studying literature in graduate school, I woke up one morning, after a night of reading some long eighteenth-century poems and a couple of tomes of Victorian prose, and thought to myself, "Wow, I could enjoy reading anything." By this point, I'd developed some tolerance for even the most inane student papers—for which the aspiring authors were grateful, though they grew to doubt my word when I'd say, "You're going to love this story we're reading today." They came to realize that I could love anything made of words, or at least find interest in it;. With some justice, they suspected that I could gleefully analyze the cereal box over breakfast.

Something similar happens with geographers, birdwatchers, rock hounds, animal lovers, and all varieties of nature aficionados. Their ability to appreciate a landscape grows until even the vacant lots on wasted city blocks hold interest. A skinny brown-striped sparrow, the dullest of birds, offers a challenge in identification. The path a possum leaves beside a road becomes a portal to a land of wonder. At some point, their capacity for boredom shrinks to the point of atrophy.

I'm sure some people will think that's the way it is with me and the Brazos Valley: Starved for breathless mountain scenery or sublime seascapes, I've learned to live with what falls before my eyes—and even love it. By now, you're thinking, this guy cannot be trusted. He can find value in a worn-out cotton field and meditate on a roadkilled rabbit. His claims for this place he calls home have to be overstated.

But that's not the way it is.

Anyone who thinks it is, try this. Drive southwest

out of Huntsville on a fine winter day after lunch. Put the prison and the interstate traffic behind you. Stop in the Sam Houston National Forest and walk one of the trails for an hour or so, just to let your brain and your eye get adjusted to the subtle things outdoors. A walk with soft pine litter under foot and the gray-brown forest birds twittering in the quiet of the relatively abandoned place makes for excellent decompression after a month of office work, television, and Internet surfing. Breathe in the pine-scented air. Have some water; maybe eat an apple.

Now, with your mind and senses prepared, drive northwest toward Anderson, Texas. Watch the land begin to rise and roll, the late afternoon sun slanting golden over the flaxen grasses of the prairies, the cattle milling in the fields, the more numerous winter hawks and ever-present black vultures catching the updrafts of a steady wind, the domes of bright land cut and sculpted by creeks running fast to catch the Navasota on its headlong pursuit of the Brazos, the stands of oak and cedar offering relief and emphasis to the spread of the prairie.

I doubt that even the most jaded eye could miss the beauty of this place. Feel free to reject my recommendation of a long poem or book of thick prose. But trust me on this.

One beautiful morning in late winter, Gentry and I are out on a photographic expedition to Lick Creek Park just south of College Station, a nice patch of post-oak savanna with trails maintained by the city. It's about fifty degrees, the sun just up.

We've barely walked fifty yards—me with the equipment bag, Gentry following with the camera and tripod—when a glimmer of special light catches in the corner of my eye. By the time I turn to see the dew glinting off clumps of silvery gossamer grass standing out against the contrasting bronze of another variety, Gentry is already heading that way and opening the legs of the tripod.

He moves here and there, testing the light, showing me what he sees in the viewfinder, then shifting as the sun rises, changing the scene with each new position in the sky. He takes a few shots, never quite satisfied. He tells me that what he remembers most fondly about the book of photographs he did on the Big Bend National Park was the appearance of that bold world through the viewfinder, the framing and focusing, the promise of the picture more than the outcome. It was at this time that he could feel, hear, and smell the environment as he was viewing the image for the first time.

We pack up and complete the two-mile loop at our leisurely pace, taking a couple of hours for Gentry to try his luck at capturing the movement of winter wetness through the groves of trees. At one point, he focuses on the eroded trail and gets a nice shot of what looks like an aerial view of an alluvial plain in miniature.

On our way out, we pass again by the grassy opening at the trailhead. Now it's in full sun, the dew burned off. The silver and bronze have disappeared, leaving a plain brown field of grassy ground that anybody could walk right past without any reason to notice. As luck would have it, the photograph didn't turn out well. "Sometimes the magic just doesn't work," Gentry told me. I guess you had to be there.

Frederick Law Olmsted, the father of landscape architecture in the New World, the designer of New York's Central Park, wrote a nice long book about a saddle trip he took across Texas from 1855 to 1856. He followed the Texas portions of the old Spanish Camino Real that ran from Florida to San Antonio and on to the City of Mexico. Like many travelers of that era, he found the east Texas Piney Woods boring after a hundred miles—as unrelenting and dull as the pork and cornpone diet of the people there, he said.

Olmsted welcomed the more open vistas that greeted him as he crossed the Brazos. He admired the wide fertile bottomland and remarked on the beauty of the alternating prairies and woodlands west of the river. This famous literary tourist liked the look of the place, but like so many others, he kept riding, searching for the romance of the Far West.

To approximate his route by car, you can catch the Old San Antonio Road (OSR) by turning west from Highway 6 north of Bryan. It merges with Highway 21 just before you cross the Brazos, and then you're on your way to the major cities in that direction: Austin and San Antonio.

After a good spread of cotton fields and oil rigs in the bottomland, the land begins to rise away from the river. The incline breaks as the different creeks running to the Brazos intervene, such as the three branches of the Yegua, but the upward trend doesn't really conclude until you get almost to Austin.

I drove this route at least once a week for five years when Jackie was working in Austin. In all that time, I didn't pay much attention to the prevailing upsweep of the land. If I went by way of Bastrop, I did notice the big stand of "lost pines" that intrudes upon the sandier soil, announcing a change of terrain as you come upon the Colorado River. If I went by way of Elgin on Highway 290, I noticed that just west of that town, as you cross what seems a low ridge, a great vista opens up westward with the Balcones Escarpment on the horizon, the limestone ridge along the fault line that borders the Hill Country.

At both of these points, the crossings at Bastrop and Elgin, you seem to have entered a new world, more open and slightly brighter; the sky gets bigger, the air drier. By the time you reach I-35 running north and south along the fault line, the country has dispelled any doubt that you're in the Southwest rather than the South. The in-between land of the Brazos Valley lies behind you.

Having recently made the trips east and west out of the Bryan–College Station area, with eyes newly sensitized to the presence of the river, I now grasp a sublime fact. Even in a car rushing along at seventy miles per hour, you can allow yourself to feel the influence of the river on the wedge of land given mainly to farm and ranch between Huntsville with its big prison and Austin with its big government. The river gives the land its shape, the upward trend in both directions. In centuries of wandering through this land, it has deposited the alkaline clays and other soils that favor the oaks and open prairies between the great Piney Woods eastward and the pine-fringed ridge running from Elgin to Bastrop, beyond which the West awaits.

The river remains the ruling spirit in the Brazos Valley despite the long-term presence of people with their axes and oxen, oil drills and asphalt, automobiles and aspirations.

If you keep going south at Hempstead where Highway 6 makes a hard left toward Prairie View and Houston to the east, you come to the southern edge of the Brazos Valley, just north of Interstate 10. Here you'll find San Felipe, the original Texas home of Stephen Austin, Jane Long, William Travis, and other luminaries of local history, now a tiny community on the banks of the river.

Next to the historical markers and a pair of reconstructed buildings, one of which claims to be an accurate representation of Austin's cabin with bricks from the original chimney, fences mark locally owned land. We watch a billy goat climb a tree in a woodsy little pasture enclosed by barbed wire and a low electric fence. The tree he climbs leans diagonally over the ground, and seeing him looking back at us from ten feet in the air, and then noticing his mate on the branch just below, we decide the electric bill is a good investment.

We walk down to the river by the road, and there it is, like an old friend. "It's the same," Jackie says. But it seems to me like an old friend who's put on a few miles since you saw him last. Deeper-seeming, a little wider, with a stronger tendency to spread, but yes, the same old friend, lined with the fringe of willows and cottonwoods. Somewhat vinier in these parts, wild grapes send thick tendrils in all directions. But the channel is regular as usual, the forthright transport of the tons of water, the Navasota, the Yegua, and the other tributaries swallowed and digested along the way, determined now to get home and hold communion with the sea.

Over in the Stephen F. Austin State Park, we walk down to the mud flats by the river, following the Cottonwood Trail. The expanse of the muddy ground is impressive. Little over an hour's drive to the north, at Washington-on-the-Brazos, we had to climb down a sizable bank to reach the mud, but here the trail slopes right into it. The weight of the big cottonwood trees drives them mudward. Many have fallen.

It's a hog's paradise, but we see no sign of that animal. We do see six trees swarming with turkey vultures, the largest roost either one of us has ever seen—at least fifty, maybe a hundred birds. We come upon a group of ten deer on the way out. They seem tame as can be, virtually posing for our admiration. Driving out of the park, we see an equally large group grazing like livestock on the golf course. Only one or two even bother to look up at us. The ears come up, but not the white tails of warning. A car of tourists. No threat at all.

We drive up onto the interstate highway, cars and trucks hurtling past, heading east to Houston. Where we cross the river and look out the side window southward, we see what it has to negotiate before it can reach the Gulf: a mighty expanse of coastal plain, flat and wide all the way to the southern horizon, its low brush and brown grass pinkish in the setting sun.

Back up the valley, anyone can see that Texas A&M and its hometown keep getting bigger, spreading out and claiming new fields. A radio announcer in town calls Bryan/College Station "the Aggieplex," and with slightly more moderate wit, the Chamber of Commerce promotes the "twin cities." We may not be ready yet to compete for population with our Minnesota counterpart, but we do hear talk, with all the growth south of town, that we might become a bedroom community for North Houston.

Not yet, though.

A local politician recently said, "The Brazos Valley deserves an interstate highway." I would say that maybe we deserve a place free of the wild speed and heavy truck traffic that comes along with super highways.

So again, not yet, please.

I heard another politico suggest that we need to think of our abundant water not only as a resource but as a commodity, something we can sell to big cities like San Antonio and even Los Angeles whose thirsty populations tend to use up their natural allotment of moisture more and more quickly all the time.

I would say, not so fast. Remember what the stunted oaks tell you about the possibility of drought.

These well-meaning public servants want to modernize the Brazos Valley. They want to bring us speed and money. Get there faster and sell everything you can. Improved "quality of life," bigger opportunities, riches in retirement, some version of the promised land. Utopia, they call it—the modern heaven.

But remember that *utopia* literally means "no place," and that maybe an in-between place like the Brazos Valley today, or even an out-of-the-way place, is better than no place.

So leave the bumpy roads and flooded fields, the big university in its converted cow pasture, the snakes on the front porch and hogs in the highway, the long summer's heat and relentless humidity, the geese honking overhead in the change of the season, the winter fog. Let the tourists stop and take pictures of their children in the oceans of bluebonnets come springtime. Let the old Aggies fill the stadium for football games every fall. Then let them head on to Austin, Houston, Dallas, San Antonio for a night on the town, unbounded commercial opportunities, and a consumer paradise.

You can look for me on the muddy banks of the river, watching the colors in the water change where the willows hang low. Or puzzling over the meaning of a roadkilled raccoon, ignoring the traffic noise in a patch of post-oak woods, marveling at the brightness of the yaupon berries and the twitter of a sparrow's song.

Back home in the Brazos Valley.

Brazos Valley Images

By D. Gentry Steele

The photographs in this book are images I have made in the Brazos Valley over a number of years. Photographing nature seems always to have been a part of me—making photographs, thinking about making photographs, and looking at other photographers' photographs. Having the inclinations of a naturalist, I usually photographed the natural landscape. When I first arrived in the Brazos Valley, my tendency was to go elsewhere to photograph places well known for their visual power and beauty—places that inspired me and recharged my spiritual batteries. But slowly, as I came to know the Brazos Valley, I began to appreciate its overlooked, typically subtle, and often ephemeral strength and beauty.

The character of the region is defined by the Brazos River, the Valley's rich soils, the warm climate, plentiful rain, and high humidity. The Valley and its borderlands of rolling hills are blanketed by a patchwork of mixed woodlands and prairies, and all are dissected by the Brazos, Little Brazos, Navasota, and Little rivers and their tributaries. We, too, have shaped the face of the land, as we have come to live and raise families in the Brazos Valley. To support ourselves we have timbered woodlands and dammed streams. We have drained wetlands. We have changed prairies into plowed fields and pastures. We have transformed old wagon trails connecting small villages into six-lane highways connecting us to the rest of the world. And we stand in wonder as we watch our cities grow, plastering the valley floor with rebar and cement.

Looking more carefully, however, I have grown aware of how we and the Brazos Valley have adapted to one another. I began to notice this as I photographed nature scapes in urban areas. Our parks are a melding of indigenous woodlands and exotic plants that forms a plant community unique to our homeland. Our landscaped yards also reflect the partnership of the indigenous and exotic, the natural and the cultured. We and the wildlife have also made some adjustments to one another through time. Some animals have gone extinct, or they no longer live here. Others have survived our coming. Some have even prospered in the humanized habitats of the Valley. And we have added to the animal community, sometimes knowingly and sometimes inadvertently.

It is this rural and urban natural world of rivers and land, plants and animals, that has held my attention over the years and is the substance of this collection of photographs. The Valley does not have the dramatic beauty and power of special places such as the Grand Canyon, the Tetons, or the High Sierra. But I believe our Valley has its own strength and beauty. It is there, but I have had to find it and recognize it. Rarely do vistas reveal the strength of the Brazos Valley. Rather, the special place may be an unassuming corner of a backyard garden that glows in just the right light of a late afternoon, or it may be along the Brazos River's edge on a foggy morning. The place may be a farmhouse among rows of cotton waiting to be picked. It may be a flash of lightning in a summer storm. The power of the place may be revealed for an instant only, as a snake slides through the leaves at our feet, or in the chatter of a squirrel, or the flight of a butterfly. Most often these places are revealed in the filtered light falling on a forest floor, or in the defining light of the early morning or late evening sun. Finding these places and remembering them has added a richness to my time in the Brazos Valley.

The Brazos River & Its Tributaries

Early morning fog on the Brazos River
Burleson County

High water in the Brazos River at early ferry crossing
Washington County

(At left) Falls on the Brazos
Falls County

East Mill Creek
Washington County

Water plant in sunlight
Brazos County
Photo by Patricia L. Steele

(Following spread) Sunrise on the Brazos
Brazos County

Remnants of Ferguson's crossing on the Navasota River Brazos County

(At left) Pond reflecting late afternoon clouds Washington County

Alligator
Brazoria County

(At left) Spider lilies along bottomlands
of the Navasota River
Brazos County

Point bar and cutbank
Brazos County

(At right) Late afternoon sun on Roans Prairie
Grimes County

(Following spread) Flooded bottomland
along the Navasota River
Brazos County

White egret feeding
Brazos County

Prairies & Woodlands of the Brazos Valley

The last leaves of autumn
Brazos County

American beautyberry bush
Brazos County

Prairie land dotted with colonies of pink buttercups
Washington County

Late afternoon sun on prairie pastureland
Williamson County

(At left) Lone trees in late afternoon light
Brazos County

Speckled king snake
Brazos County

Bluebonnets, paintbrushes, and rail fence
Washington County

The first leaves of spring
Brazos County

Fox squirrels eating yaupon berries Brazos County

Post oaks and grassland
Brazos County

Brazos Valley Weather

Approaching thunderstorm
Brazos County

Post oak in fall colors capped by winter's ice storm
Brazos County

Lightning during summer storm
Brazos County

Autumn floodwaters at sunset encased in winter ice
Brazos County

(At right) Yaupon berries encased in ice
Brazos County

Clearer weather to the west at sunset
Milam County

The Human Touch on the Brazos Valley

Cotton field ready to be picked
Brazos County

Farm buildings in Brazos bottomland
Brazos County

Longhorn
Brazos County

Cemetery and old juniper Lee County

Old train trestle over the Brazos River
Brazos County

(Following spread) New highway bridge over Brazos River
Brazos County

Mature cornfield
Brazos County

Bluebonnets and abandoned early twentieth-century service station
Washington County

Road dust raised by pickup truck
Brazos County

Farm shed and trees on a late winter afternoon
Brazos County

(Following spread) Spring planting of sorghum and natural gas well
Brazos County

Hay bales in field
Burleson County

Rain clouds and plowed field
Brazos County

Carolina wren at yard birdbath
Brazos County

Butterfly on lantana
Brazos County

The Brazos Valley Imprint

Texas A&M University in an early autumn morning fog
Brazos County

Swallowtail butterfly on red flowers
Brazos County

Raindrops on a nandina plant
Brazos County

Carolina anole in a ligustrum bush
Brazos County

(At right) Shady resting spot near the old
Carnegie library, Bryan, Texas
Brazos County

Day lilies after a spring shower
Brazos County

(At left) Gulf Coast toad emerging
from its daytime shelter
Brazos County

Texas A&M University's Research Park illuminated by park lights and setting sun
Brazos County

Irises in a small pond
Brazos County

Weeping willow
in a park
Brazos County

Acknowledgments

M. Jimmie Killingsworth

For the opportunity to work on this stimulating project, I thank Shannon Davies, who provided wisdom and guidance from her long and deep experience as an editor of nature writing; Mary Lenn Dixon, who showed faith; and all of the staff at Texas A&M University Press, who have helped to make this the best possible book. I am grateful to Gentry Steele for his graciousness and inspiration as a coauthor and photographic artist. My thanks go also to all the local naturalists and historians who helped me, especially my colleague in the Texas A&M History Department, Professor Walter Buenger, my neighbor the horticulturalist Dan Lineberger, and the Brazos Valley Chapter of Texas Master Naturalists, of which I am a proud member. As always my first readers and most loving critics have been my wife and frequent coauthor Jacqueline Palmer and my daughter, the artist and writer Myrth Killingsworth.

D. Gentry Steele

First, I want to express my appreciation for my wife, Patty Steele. Her love of nature is intense and real, and we have journeyed over much of the state and the American West following this shared interest. Patty was my friend and constant companion on a previous project to photograph Big Bend National Park, and she has been my companion and driver on most of my outings in the Brazos Valley. On occasions she has photographed as well, and I am pleased to include one of her images in the book. On many of these outings, she has pointed out potential locales when I was looking the other way. Her advice to "stop and look behind you" has served me well over the years—at least on those occasions I remember to do it. I also had the pleasure of having my daughter Heather accompany me on one of my image-hunting afternoons.

My thanks are also extended to the many friends who have accompanied and guided me as I have wandered about the Brazos Valley and the many others who, during a conversation, have shared with me special places they have found.

Thanks are extended to Joel Kitchens, Mac Bradford, Tom Marshall, and Rickey Ferguson for their advice and support in photographic matters.

New friendships at the Texas A&M University Press have been formed and previous friendships have been strengthened during the preparation of this book. Shannon Davies suggested that Jimmie and I join efforts in presenting our images of the Brazos Valley, and she has been a steadfast source of encouragement and support. The enthusiastic support for the project by Charles Backus, director of the press, and the rest of the staff has made the process of turning a collection of photos into an integrated portrait of the Brazos Valley fun and personally satisfying. Their support was particularly appreciated on those days when images I had seen or photographed did not survive translation to a print. Finally, I wish to thank Mary Ann Jacob, who I believe has designed a book that frames our images in the best possible light, and Kevin Grossman, whose effort has ensured that the prints in the book are accurate recreations of the images I envisioned.

To all of these friends, I thank you.

Reflections of the Brazos Valley
was composed into a book
with a Macintosh computer
using 12 point Fairfield LH Light font
with 16 points of spacing between lines.
The book was designed by Mary Ann Jacob,
typeset by Kevin Grossman,
printed and bound by Everbest Printing Co.
through Four Colour Imports.
The paper on which this book is printed,
157 gsm Goldeast Matte Art White,
carries acid-free characteristics
for an effective life
of at least three hundred years.

TEXAS A&M UNIVERSITY PRESS
COLLEGE STATION

ISBN-13: 978-1-58544-615-5
ISBN-10: 1-58544-615-7
52500
9 781585 446155